Crumble the Old Man

Written by

Birdella A. Tucker

Copyright August 2017
ISBN 13: 9781975799731
ISBN 10: 1975799739

All Scripture is from KJV

Contact information
birdie tucker@hotmail.com

Upon This Mountain, The Lord Shall Reign...

Introduction

Psalm 85:10" Love and Loyalty now meet, Righteousness and Peace now embrace, and Righteousness leans down from heaven, Yahweh Himself bestows happiness as our soul gives its harvest, Righteousness always preceding him and Peace following His footsteps.

God's love and loyalty, His righteousness and peace, met with our spirit at the Cross. The Holy Spirit now comes to reveal areas in our soul that need to go through the process of death, burial (separation from our mind, will, and emotions) to meet with the Father in resurrection life. This new life is a life after His character, His nature, His love, and His peace. Without the joining, our iniquities bar His presence from our soul.

Each encounter with our soul is like confronting a mountain, which is a hindrance to our abiding in Him. These mountains are strongholds. Our job, "Climb that mountain and cause the mountains of the flesh to crumble." As I write this, I have a vivid image of the soldiers erecting the flag of the United States on Iwo Jima. The raising of the flag indicated that the United States captured the mountain. We, too, are climbing mountains. After we defeat the enemies, we must lift up the name of Jesus

Christ as Lord over the things we conquered. We fight this war, not with flesh and blood but with the Blood of Jesus.

Acknowledgement

To Pastor Ataloa Woodin.

While at Pastor Ataloa's bible study, she turned to me and said, *"You are to write a book and call it "Crumble the Old Man."* Out of obedience, I immediately went home, turned on my computer, and wrote out the title. I was staking my claim to a new book.

Chapter 1
Cannibalism

"Having abolished in his flesh the enmity, even the law of commandments contained in ordinances: for to make in himself of twain one new man, so making peace showing that we have been reconciled back to the Father. Jesus destroyed the enmity called sin, so that we might become one with the Father and the Son and the Holy Spirit."

The very first command that God gave to us was, *"Be fruitful and replenish the earth,"* stands as a monument to the mountains ahead of us. Each mountain (our flesh) in which we conquer, a flag of victory is planted in the kingdom. Jesus made us conquerors in His name. Our job is to take His name and His authority to enforce His commands. There are to be no sluggards. It takes work to crumble our flesh and work to establish His plans by faith. Like anything else in the world, there is a price to pay or a cost. What is the cost you ask? The cost is seeing our old mindset crumble when faced with the truth. What is the truth? It is Jesus Christ in us, our hope of glory. Without establishing His Truth as the flag over the mountains, we remain in bondage to a lie.

A carnal person believes the lie that God will accept any

sacrifice that he makes as long as he worked hard. When his sacrifice is not accepted, he is left with thoughts and emotions against those who offer God the sacrifice required, which is the blood of Jesus. Only His blood can destroy sin and change the carnal mind into the mind of Christ. This is what Cain did. He worked hard to offer to God the works of his hands only to learn that God did not accept his sacrifice. Abel, on the other hand, offered to God the blood of a lamb, to which God showed respect. Cain, feeling rejected, turned his heart to hating his brother, and devised a plan to kill him.

"And in process of time it came to pass, that Cain brought of the fruit of the ground an offering unto the LORD. And Abel, he also brought of the firstlings of his flock and of the fat thereof. And the LORD had respect unto Abel and to his offering (Genesis 4:3-4).

This book, Crumble the Old Man, is a diary of the works of my flesh that needed to be crucified in Jesus. I write this not to excuse my sacrifices but to reveal that the power of the Blood to set me free from my flesh. Without repentance for the works of our hands, there is no remission. Our work then, become self-seeking, a delusion. What this means is this: If I am to have the mind of Christ and have my soul quickened to be like Him, then I have to learn what He expects from me.

When I was a child, one of my sacrifices that I made was self-protection. I was taught that the best defense was an effective offense. Like Cain, who wanted to protect himself from feeling rejected, I would deal with rejection by either being outward aggressive toward others or retreat into my soul as an introvert in order to protect my feelings. As long as I used these methods to protect myself, I failed to give glory to God as being my protector. My actions revealed that I did not respect His sacrifice, His Son. As much as I hated to deal with these hurts and pains in my emotions, I knew that this old man had to crumble.

When we are under the lie that God does not love us, we act as Cain and wander in wilderness places. We desire to be in God's presence and receive His favors but unless we accept the truth, that God loves us and has already accepted us as His, we choose to allow our flesh to rule. We have made our ways our god.

The other night I saw a picture regarding cannibalism. One man was eating the flesh of another. I can still hear my response, "How gross!" Then I heard a word, "mistake." When I awoke, I asked the Holy Spirit to explain to me what the meaning of this dream meant. I was told that I was afraid of making a mistake and afraid of someone telling me that I did something wrong. As a result, I began to criticize others who made mistakes and bashed myself. Criticism was an act of feeding on the flesh. It is dead works. It is cannibalism.

I looked up the word cannibalism and learned that doctors made a study on those who in actuality ate the bodies of dead humans. The protein in the body of the dead person carries a prion. A prion is a type of protein that can trigger normal proteins in the brain to fold abnormally. It is also known as GSS disease that attacks the brain cells and keeps them from working, or in connecting the proper impulses in the brain to the body. In other words, an enmity between the mind and the body has occurred. Because of this separation, the body becomes hostel to other parts of the body. The body then creates an autoimmune system in which the body turns on itself.

Prion is noted for the root cause of Parkinson's, Alzheimer's, and other diseases affecting the nervous system. Here comes the good news. Jesus abolished the enmity that separated us from His presence. Therefore, the results of Prion can be destroyed because the Blood of Jesus broke all forms of cannibalism, even self-hatred or criticism. In this book, we will discuss several mountains that need to crumble.

Chapter 2
The Need to Understand

I can remember looking at this mountain of needing to understand as if it was yesterday. My parents moved to a small town called Tamales in hopes of finding a job for my father. Tamales is a small dairy community along the Pacific Coast. My father was an out of work contractor needing to find something in which he thought he could support the family. He found a five-acre parcel of land with a small house along the road-side and a chicken coop located in the back. With the land came a few dairy cows and one horse. The family moved into the house and my grandmother moved into the chicken coop. The land was bordered on one side by Eucalyptus trees, and on another side, Mayflower apples.

I would sit in the apple tree, (I was about 10 years old) eating an apple, of course, and would yell out, *"I love you God, but I don't know you."* I was confident that no one would hear me, as we were *"In the Boondocks."* I noticed that my words would echo back to me in some form, so this got my attention. Repeatedly I would yell, *"I love you, God."*

Whether it was the echo or God's Spirit that got my

attention, I do not know. However, a desire entered my heart and like a little bird ready to receive the worms from his mother, my mouth was open to receive His love.

My grandmother was a deaconess in her church, the SDA, or Seventh Day Adventist Church. It was her desire to teach us all that she had learned. That is good. The only trouble was that she was afraid that if we did not keep the Sabbath, which we did not, we would go to hell. Prompted by the fear of hell and her desire to save us, she asked my father if she could teach us the Bible. I did not mind the bible stories. In fact, I liked them. Especially those from the Old Testament. I saw God as my champion, my defender, my protector. All was well, until the "*law of do's and don'ts entered.*" When I was told it was sin to eat pork, sin to go to a show, sin to have caffeine, sin to work on Saturday, etc, I balked. I could not identify with this "god." Instead of seeing God's goodness, I saw my failures and inabilities to comply with the rules. I remembered the old saying, "*the best defense is an effective offense.*" I became offensive toward my grandmother, and she knew it. I felt inept, offended, unworthy, and unaccepted.

Therefore, at the very beginning of my climb up the mountain of the need to understand, I fumbled. I did not want Bible studies any more. Fortunately, we moved to Santa Rosa where I met my life-long friend, Lee. She attended the Southern Baptist Church and invited me to Vacation Bible School. I loved it. They spoke of a loving Jesus who loved me enough to die for me. When asked if I wanted to know this Jesus, I ran to the front of the church. I wanted to understand how to be saved and what it meant to be "saved."

Well, after a short time living in Santa Rosa, my dad was out of work again and we moved to Centerville where Dad got a job operating an asphalt plant. I felt the emptiness in my heart once again. I decided to give the Adventist Church another chance. After all, I was older now (in high school) and could better understand things. I wanted to have fellowship with God, so I consented to go to church thinking, maybe if I tried harder, I could understand God better. Within a couple of weeks, I was reacting again. Instead of finding peace in my soul, I became angry at what I was being taught and angry with my grandmother again. For the next four years, I concentrated on schoolwork. I wanted to understand knowledge and excel. I had some "highs," especially when I would get an "A," but that did not last, as it was only mental excitement and not the joy of knowing God.

By the time I was seventeen, my hunger for God

increased. I would cry out, again, "*God I love you, but I don't know you.*" As God would have it, Billy Graham came to Fresno. I was excited about the crusade. I knew that I had to go, no matter what. My brother, Byron, decided that he wanted Jesus in his heart also, so we both went to the Fresno Stadium where the event was held. We were late in getting there, so we ended up practically in the back row. Billy Graham looked so far away, yet God was close. When the invitation came to rededicate my life to Jesus, once again I ran forward, much like I did at the Southern Baptist Church in Santa Rosa. I was given a pamphlet on St. John to study. At the end of the pamphlet were questions that I was to answer and return the answers to the place indicated. This was good for a while, but I needed fellowship with God. I did not just want to answer questions about God. I wanted to know Him.

During my high school years, I clung to the one thing that I remembered in Tamales, God is my protector, my provider, and He loves me. With these feelings, I believed that nothing could ever harm me.

I loved God, but had a lack of knowledge about God. In my mind, He would not let anything harm me. My thinking was far from being mature. I would do some very stupid things, like ride on top of the back seat of Byron's convertible singing to God and playing my trumpet. Years later, I would cringe thinking what could have happened to me if Byron had suddenly slammed on the breaks, or if we were in an accident. It never entered my mind that I could ever be harmed, *"I was in love with God."*

I remember a time in which I almost drowned. Byron, myself, and others from school would float down the Kings River in an inner tube. It was so much fun that we would do it over and over again in one day. Never did we think that during the evening the manager of the dam would open up the head gates and let more water flow down the river. Well, he did, and we were caught in a rapid flow of water that overturned my inner tube. When the surge of water hit my tube, I was thrown upside down and under water. One of the kids near me grabbed my tube and waited for me to bob to the surface. That was the last time I was in the river. I learned a lesson the hard way.

About a year after the Billy Graham Crusade, I met my husband to be, George. A short time after our marriage, we moved out to the country near Campbell Mountain. My cry to know God began to rise even stronger. I would ask Him, *"How do I get to know you, God. Are there books about you? Where are these books?"* Not knowing how to find these books, I started to read the Bible.

For the next fifty-six years, I attended Bible studies, went to crusades, Bible College, training sessions, etc., and found many books about God in order to know Him. It was not until 2017, that things changed. The Holy Spirit asked me to lay down the ways I attempted to understand God in order to receive the Spirit of Understanding, spoken in Isaiah 11.

As I was praying with a friend, the Lord told her that I blamed God for something that happened to me in the past. I heard a Word, Isaiah 6:9. *"And he said, Go, and tell this people, Hear ye indeed, but understand not; and see ye indeed, but perceive not."* Well, I did not understand what the Lord wanted to tell me, so I went to sleep. The next morning, while in prayer, it was as if the cloud of "not understanding" was removed. Understanding comes from God's Spirit of knowing Him, His character, nature, and power. When we do not know Him and receive Him into our spirit, soul, and body, we attempt to climb the mountain of understanding and the need to understand by our flesh. Paul addresses this in Galatians. As long as we are but a child, we need a tutor. However, when we mature, we let go of the tutor and take our place in Christ to hear from His Spirit. I spoke again to God, this time to humble myself and place my need to understand at the foot of the Cross. I received the fact that all of God dwells within me but as long as I walk in my own abilities to understand, a shroud of darkness separated us.

After I did this, I understood that I had blamed God for not protecting me from an accident in 1965. If He was my protector, where was He? I tried to understand why I was in an accident. Had I done something wrong or was there some sin that I had committed as was being punished. In my need to understand, I sought out to understand the doors that I opened to allow the enemy to enter. The thief came to steal my love toward God and from knowing His love for me. As I write this, The Spirit reminded me of a word Jesus told Peter. Satan desired to sift him as wheat, but that God was praying for him. I was being sifted, but God has been praying for me all of this time.

Chapter 3
Climb for Holiness

In the early 80 I felt called to the ministry. I was on fire for God and ready to serve Him with all of my might and dogged determination. After experiencing an accident in which one of my fingers were cut off and the other one cut in half, I had a dream. In this dream, I was climbing the mountain to enter God's presence. At the top of the mountain I came to a roadblock. I could either force my way through the blockade or ascend down and make a detour up another way. If I went down, I would pass through a swamp. While in the swamps, I felt the filth and my reaction to the filth. My skin felt like it was crawling, but I was determined to enter into the place called "Holy." I knew that the swamp was a slough of sins and iniquities that I wanted to leave. My interpretation of the dream was Psalm 15.

"Lord, who may dwell in our sacred tent? Who may live on your holy mountain? The one whose walk is blameless, who does what is righteous, who speaks the truth from their heart; whose tongue utters no slander, who does no wrong to a neighbor, and casts no slur on others; who despises a vile person but honors those who fear the LORD; who keeps an oath even when it hurts, and does not change their mind; who lends

money to the poor without interest; who does not accept a bribe against the innocent. Whoever does these things will never be shaken."

I concluded that in order to be with a holy God, I had to address all the iniquities and sin in my life first, bring them to the Cross in repentance, and then I could enter the Holy of Holies.

Well, I continued on this "quest" for over thirty years. Each time the Holy Spirit revealed a sin within my soul; I would repent and experience God's presence.

One day, my friend, Mary, had a dream. She said she saw me going through the mud to get to Jesus, but that there was another way. When she told me the dream, I presented it to the Lord and waited for instructions. Month's passed before I felt that I had a visitation from God. I was entering the Holy Place with clean hands all right, because I repented of sin; but Jesus already presented His blood and declared me clean to the Father. Instead of going up the mountain as the priests did in the Old Testament, Jesus presented me righteous and placed me at the Father's right hand in Him. The difference is this: Jesus made me righteous and has already cleansed me with His Blood. From that position, being seated in

Him, I am to look down at my flesh and crucify it.

I really had a hard time receiving this. Surely, I had to repent first, and then I would be able to enter God's presence, verses receiving His holiness in my spirit first, and then deal with my soul. Had I not had a divine dream that I would have to make a detour in my ascent to the Holy Place?

At a Bible Study called Kingdom New Man by Currie Blake, I read that God will permit what I permit. At the time of the dream in the 80's, I only knew the teachings that sin could not enter God's presence, so I addressed sin. As I journeyed on my "Quest," I came to a place of receiving the gift of being accepted first, then I could deal with the things that do not please God. We are to walk as Enoch with God. In the relationship, if I do something that offends God's character and nature, I need to ask His forgiveness as it breaks our fellowship and grieves His Spirit.

"Sin Consciousness" was a mountain that needed to crumble. Because it was such a big part of my upbringing, it was a hard-long journey. The letting go of my determination to walk with God in holiness began to crumble when I saw that God desires for me to walk with

Him as He walked with Adam in the Garden.

Chapter 4
The Tongue

The tongue has the power to speak life or death. With the tongue, we can glorify God by speaking that which He has already spoken, or we can speak words from darkness. No man can control it, as it is un-unruly member of the body. The tongue has to be delivered. The tongue stands as a mountain to hinder us from receiving God's goodness.

Those who speak God's Words walk with God. Those who speak negative words are bound to a low-life existence. For years I would try to control my tongue from speaking out the fears that had me bound. I was not the only one in my family bound by the power of the tongue. A negative spirit controlled my husband's tongue. If something was black, he would say it was white. George was afraid to speak God's Word as he was afraid of failure, so speaking the opposite of the Word kept him from fear of not receiving. My reaction to these words, after knowing that life and death were in the power of the tongue, was to become angry with him. I thought Satan was using George's words to curse us and keep us in bondage. I did not realize that the curse causeless shall not come to those who know who they are

n Christ. If I receive the words of Jesus, that I am joint-
heirs with Him, righteous and redeemed, I would not
have feared the words that came out of George's mouth.
The only way to crumble this mountain was to
understand that I am already redeemed from the curse.

A couple of days after starting this book, three things
happened. First, a friend asked me to pray for her as she
went to share the Word of God to an unsaved person. I
prayed as I said I would, but I did not receive a report on
this person's visit until I awoke the next day, only to find
on my phone a txt, *"Let the redeemed of the Lord say so."*
The second thing that happened was that I had a dream
about Israel wanting to return to the leeks and the garlic
of Egypt.

The third thing that happened was that my husband
started cursing God for everything. George was afraid of
not having enough money, so he blamed God. My
reaction was aggressive. I commanded him to shut up
and expressed my anger to the words he was saying. I
knew that my response was wrong, so I repented and
asked God to help me. This mountain (reacting to curse
words, had to crumble. I felt that the dream I had held a
clue to what I was facing. Turning to the Scriptures, to my
surprise, I read in Numbers 11:5 that the children of Israel

wanted to return to Egypt when things did not go their way because the leeks and the garlic did not cost them anything. Wow! Fear of lack, fear of having to lay down the flesh, fear of fighting the enemy and demanding that someone pay for the pain George was having in his body opened the door to curse God. George believed the lie that it was God's fault. He refused to either see the thief, Satan, or see that he refused to forgive others who had disappointed him.

When we are hurt and demand that someone pays for hurting us, we inadvertently reject the price Jesus paid to set us free. Jesus paid the price for all offenses and hurts. When we reject what He did, we open the door to return to Egypt. In death, a person can speak words of death (murmuring and complaining) without feeling guilty. Egypt offers us "rights" to feel hurt and desire vengeance on those who have hurt us.

God, in His grace, had given me the words to speak from the txt that I had received. *"Let the redeemed of the Lord say so."* I began to say, *"Tongue! You have been redeemed by the blood of the Lamb." "You will speak life and not death."* I began to take authority over this mountain of ... (everything the tongue speaks) and command it to crumble by the power of the Word in Proverbs 31, which says, a virtuous woman's family has no fear of lack. Why?

Because those in the family trusted in the person God positioned in the home. I declare that Jesus is Lord in my home and that He can be trusted. He already destroyed lack and released the blessings of provisions.

Once we know what Jesus did for us, and receive our position in Him, we begin to change the way we think and act. Walking in God's presence brings life. Listening to His Words encourages us to leave that which brings death.

Chapter 5
Dishonor

In 1953, my husband received papers from the draft board. He was eighteen and eligible to serve the United States of America. It was his honor to fight for his country. The time was the ending of the Korea War. The different branches of service were looking for young men to join their particular branch. Each branch offered incentives for those who would enlist with them and serve a four-year hitch verses a two-year obligation with the Army. What they offered was enticing. George signed on the bottom line.

The recruiting officer promised those who signed the agreement things that were not written in the G.I. Bill. We learned this years later. In George's mind, he believed the recruiter and blamed the Veteran's of Foreign Wars for not keeping their word. He was honorable to trust in America and expected our government to honor their word to him. He was to have free medical and dental services for his service.

When we were told that he was not eligible for free treatments (we had to give a "co-pay" for each service) and that dental was not included, George became angry. The lie, fear of lack, controlled him. I asked God why

George was reacting instead of trusting Him. That night, I had a dream. In the dream I saw George with 100 marbles in his hands. Little by little, people would come to George and ask him for a marble, which he gave. Slowly, all but one marble was left to George, and he was not going to let anyone take his last marble. He would fight for it if he had to. George felt that if he gave up his last marble, he would have nothing to provide for his family.

This fear had to come down, as it was a lie. God supplies all of our needs according to His riches in Christ Jesus. More than the money, George wanted to trust in people. He lived a life of honor and expected others to be honorable to him, which did not happen in his eyes.

I was sure that we could not do anything to change the system. We would just have to "suck it up." God had another plan. In Reedley, just off I Street by the old community swimming pool stands an Arc of Honor listing the Koreans who had gone to war for the United States. As soon as I faced the Arc intercession by the Holy Spirit came upon me. Lack of honor was a mountain that had to crumble, not just for us but also for all the veterans who put their lives on the line.

After the intercession, I contacted the Veterans and asked for information regarding George's status. I was assigned a representative who helped me apply for a hearing. We had to present George's discharge papers indicating that he was in the Korean War, even if it was the last day of the "conflict" and entitled to certain benefits. As a result, a doctor tested his hearing and discovered that due to George's shooting the big guns on the USS Saint Paul, a loss of hearing occurred. George was now entitled to a 10% disability that allowed him to see the doctors free of charge (No co-pay) and receive a pension of $137.00 once a month. What a difference this made in staying afloat. However, that is not all. George was being honored at last in this area.

A few months later, I had a dream in which I heard a voice speak. The voice said, *"Tell her, she has a right to know the truth."* *"Truth?"* *"What truth?"* A few days later George started bleeding from his kidneys. We took him to the Veterans again. The urologist asked me to tell him of all the surgeries George had had. When I told him about the time in which George went into the hospital to fix aneurisms in his body, and that the surgery was to take 5 hours but lasted ten, the doctor said, *"That's why the kidneys began to atrophy, lack of oxygen."*

The atrophying of the kidneys resulted in a magnitude
of physical traumas for over sixteen years. As a result, we
had to return to the Veterans almost every month in an
attempt to locate the problems that occurred in his body.
Now, the truth was known. The truth had been withheld
from us all this time. Maybe the doctors feared that we
would sue. I do not know. No one had told us the truth,
until now. Once this last doctor told me that the problem
was due to lack of oxygen, I thought to myself, "*God has
honored me by telling me the truth as to why the kidneys
failed.*"

With this truth I could speak, "*I forgive the doctors.*" The
thief came to steal George's life, but God was not caught
unaware. Honor requires honor. Going back sixteen years
when the first surgery took place to correct aneurisms in
George's veins, I had had a dream. In this dream, an
assignment of death was released against two people.
Both were given instruction in which to obey. In the
dream, I saw that the first person did not obey God's
instructions, so he died. The assignment against the
second person involved my obedience. I was told not to
eat "nutterbutter cookies." I had never heard of
nutterbutter cookies so I did not know what the dream
meant. I was however, shown the morgue at the hospital,
and felt the severity for obedience. When I awoke from
sleep, I asked God, "*What do you mean? I do not understand*

these instructions; nevertheless, I will pray in the spirit and ask You for help."

The surgery was at San Francisco Hospital. Our daughter, Traci, accompanied me and waited with me. After the surgery, when George seemed fine, Traci decided to return home. She left her back pack, filled with treats, with me. As I opened the bag, there they were, "nutterbutter cookies." I wasted no time in throwing them in the garbage. I was not going to "*reason in my mind*" for understanding. I was going to obey. I learned that the person in the recovery room with George died, which was in my dream.

Now, when we finally were told the truth when George's kidneys started to die, I rejoiced in my God again. The promise to save him at the time of surgery sixteen years earlier was connected to our present. If God saved George then, He would save George now.

I also heard a word from God's Spirit speaking to me. *"Ask Me for new kidneys and a new pluming system for George."* Because of the truth that came to me, reminding me of the nutterbutter cookies, I confronted the fear of George dying and overcame, for a season. The next eighteen years was filled with doctor visits, hospital visits, surgeries for ports to allow dialysis, etc. After one of the hospitals visits the doctors recommended that I become George's fiduciary until his mind became stable. The in lack of the kidney's function caused mental disturbances. Upon given this responsibility, I contacted President Trump at the White House and asked Him and America to forgive us for murmuring and complaining against our country. I had a legal right to use George's name. Within a week I was contacted by the Disabled American Veterans as to how they could help. I told them that George needed a fistula in his arm in which to receive dialysis. He had an emergency port placed in his chest for the time being. It has taken us about one year to prepare George for surgeries as one of the fistula's stopped working after three days. God honored my husband immediately after we repented for cursing our country. We are still crumbling this mountain of dishonor as the "old man" thinks that he has a right to grumble. No. We have a right to praise God and pray in His Word.

Chapter 6
Wrong Responses

Years ago, a friend called to tell me that I was like Queen Vashti in the Book of Esther. This really was not a compliment. Vashti's response to her husband was a mountain that ruled my life. God explained it like this. Under the spirit of self-righteousness, when someone wanted to force me to do something that was not righteous, I responded aggressively in my "not" doing it, just like Vashti, when she refused to appear naked before a bunch of men. Vashti was bold and abrupt with her response, "No!" When I know something to be wrong, I boldly declare it but with a strong response that forced others to respond in their flesh. As a result, God did not receive any glory.

I asked God, "*How could Vashti have responded differently?*" The answer was so plain. "*She could have humbled herself before God and ask Him.*" Yes, I know that God is not mentioned in the Book of Esther but a supreme Deity was. I did not have any excuses. I knew that there is a God, and His name is Jehovah. I could have even asked Jesus what to do. Then, in obedience to His direction, God would receive glory.

A few weeks before a spiritual conference, I received a word from the Lord. "Seth." Hum. *"What is God trying to tell me?"* I did the normal things, like, look up the word 'Seth" in the Bible. It means replacement. Eve said God has given her a replacement for the loss of Abel.

I believed that it was time to receive a replacement for the things that we have lost to the thief. My first thought went to marriage, finances, friends, etc. It was not until I viewed an episode from a *"Murder She Wrote"* series that something else came as a revelation to me. One of J.B. Fletcher's dearest friends, whom she loved dearly, was Dr. Seth Hazlett. Seth had an attitude and responded with negative emotions to most everything. One time, when Seth and J.B were dinning out, Seth was murmuring about the soup, the waitress, the management, and just about everything. J.B.'s response was, "Oh, Seth." She said it to him with such love and respect for her dear friend.

In this scene, another person entered the restaurant complaining, demanding her rights, and all with a loud voice. J.B.'s response to her was a sign of shame and embarrassment. J.B had never seen this woman before. She had no love attachment, no commitment. As I looked at the scene, it was as if the Holy Spirit spoke to me, saying. *"Say, 'Oh, Seth' to yourself each time someone has* a bad attitude. The reason is this: God so loved us that His attitude toward us is love, even with a greater love than J.B. had for Seth. I was to replace the bad responses with responses of love. I was not to allow my flesh to respond. I was to say to myself, "*Oh, Seth.*"

I was so excited with this revelation that I shared it with my friends. Their assignment was, when something starts to arouse a bad response, they were to say, "Oh, Seth."

Chapter 7
The Con

Someone who con's another is one who persuades them to believe something that is not true. This person is adept in lying. I hated to be conned. I did not like to be around some who would con. Yet, I was conned innumerous times. Sometimes, I would know that I was being conned, yet allowed the person to have power over me. Seeing my weakness, I asked God to give me the response J. B. Fletcher (Murder She Wrote), had. The guilty person would say all sorts of reason why they did not kill so and so. Jessica would comely respond, "*Yes, you did.*" She could not be conned into a lie once she knew the truth. I saw that people could con me when I was not sure what the truth was. I could think that they were wrong but a lingering thought over-rode me, "*Maybe, just maybe, they are right.*"

As I was praying about this, a revelation came regarding my desire to be a good person and help others. Jesus says, "*The goodness of God leads to repentance.*" When we do not know God's will in the things that we confront, we will doubt the voice of the Holy Spirit who speaks to warn us. I was afraid of correcting someone in a lie because I was afraid that the spirit of anger would raise its ugly head. Because of fear, I would even doubt that the Holy Spirit was warning me about the lie. This is called having a double mind. On one side, I wanted the Holy Spirit to warn me, on the other side, I was afraid of my reactions to a lie.

However, both responses were from my emotions and not from His Spirit. This mountain must crumble. It was after the flesh and not after the *"Rock from which I was hewn."* I was bowing down to a god of emotions instead of the "Rock." Probably, the desire to be liked paid a great part in my captivity.

I remembered what happened to Moses when he struck the rock instead of speaking to the rock. God was angry with him because it showed that he really did not trust God to do what He said He would do. Giving my self to a con show that I do not trust God to take control of the situation. My actions were self-exalting.

Years ago, a person came to me with a rock. He said, *"Look at the gold in this rock."* He was so sure that he had found gold that he would take off from work just to dig for gold. He was going to be rich. There was only one problem. He did not have enough money to buy food or expenses to support him while he worked the mine. That was where I came in. *"How about a loan?"* *"I'll pay you back as soon as I hit the mother-load."* I knew that, or at least thought, that what he was looking at was fools gold but I did not want to bust his bubble. Because I loved this person, I usually gave in to giving him money, only to feel that I was conned afterward. Then, I would hate myself for not being strong enough to say, "No."

What a predicament. On the one side, I was like Vashti who did not care if she hurt someone while on the other side, afraid that I would hurt someone's feelings. When we are seduced to follow our emotions, we are under a stronghold in our mind. Another spirit was in control and wanted to destroy my ability to rule over the mountains that rose up against me. I was to speak to the mountains for them to move. I was not to allow the mountains to stand as a monument to my failure to obey God. This mountain of being "conned" must crumble.

Chapter 8
Oppression

Just before George was to go again San Francisco in 2000, this time to remove his bladder, I heard a word from God. *"Build Me an altar."* The altar had to be from un-cut rocks and higher than my height. I heard the word, Isaiah 19: 19-20

"In that day shall there be an altar to the Lord in the midst of the land of Egypt, and a pillar at the border thereof to the Lord. And it shall be for a sign and for a witness unto the Lord of hosts in the land of Egypt: for they shall cry unto the Lord because of the oppressors, and he shall send them a savior, and a great one, and he shall deliver them."

That morning I received a phone call from a friend in Idaho. God told her to tell me that I was to build an altar to the Lord. It had to be from un-cut stones and higher than my height. There was no doubt that God was instructing me to do something ... build an altar to Him. The altar represented my making covenant with God against the oppressors that were attacking us. I looked up the meaning of "oppressor" and learned that it meant harsh and authoritarian, cruel and unjust treatment. Satan is a hard taskmaster. He was oppressing us with the mind to destroy us. *"But, God."* God had another plan. He knew that the years of oppression would be hard and that I needed something as a witness to look at in order to keep up my faith. This *"pile of rocks"* was just that. I would lay my hands on it many times when my spirit was low, reminding God of our covenant. I think we battled every emotion and physical ailment possible and shed gallons of tears. After several years of struggling, I heard another word from the Lord. *"You will have to confront Pharaoh.* During this time, I went to Bethel, Redding to receive ministry. In one of the sessions, I was given another word, *"You will confront a giant, like Jack in the Bean Stock. However, you will not kill him; however, you will cause him to fall in worship of God."* I put that word on the back burner of my mind as I was not quite sure if the two words were the same, Pharaoh and Jack.

About five years ago, just before George and I moved from the land in which the altar stood, I had a dream. I saw my future great grandson (who was not born yet) at about the age of three standing by his father, Tim, asking a question as he pointed to the altar. *"What is this pile of rocks, Dad."* Tim would answer, *"By reason of the oppressor, Grandma cried out to the Lord and He sent a savor to deliver them."* I told the instructions to Tim making him promise that he would speak of God's promises to his son when he had one. As I write this book, my grandson, Gage, is almost three years old. My heart begins to stir with anticipation as I remember God's promises to me.

One of the things that I think about when I think of Pharaoh is *"He hardened his heart against God."* Over the years of anguish with all of the physical, emotional, and mental hatred, I saw that George's heart had become hardened against God. He blamed Him for everything. In his mind, he was righteous and that which was happening to him was unrighteous. If God really loved him, then this would not be happening to him.

The harder his heart became against God and others, especially the doctors at the Veterans, I noticed that his heart was hardening against me, also. I fought to keep a tender heart but I noticed my heart becoming hard.

Having a hard heart was contrary to a heart of love that I had for God. My heart was divided. To a divided heart the Lord says that we will either love the one or hate the other. We have to make a choice. Listening to the words that came from George's mouth was like being oppressed. I needed a heart transplant. That is when I got the word, "*Oh, Seth.*" I would have to counteract my immediate reactions with love and forgiveness ... which is work! I asked God to give me a new heart, one after Him and not one after the flesh.

Chapter 9
Rosie the Riveter

I can still visualize seeing my mother with a bandana on her head to keep her hair from either falling in her face as she worked or to hold the curlers in place at night. You know the old adage, *"What you see is what you get."* Well, for over fifty years I would place the triangle cotton bandana over my curlers to keep them in place while I slept. This habit stayed with me even up to this date. I was never comfortable in changing to a curling iron in order to fix my hair. Old habits are hard to break.

Speaking about old habits, what Rosie represented was, *"We Can Do it!"* Because of the war, women were forced into the factories and into positions primarily held by men. They had to do it, the job, that is, as their country needed them, and the need to survive pushed them forward. Work was not considered either men's work or women's work. Work was work. Everyone was engrained with a work ethic, if you did not work, you did not eat. There was no time to coddle anyone.

The pendulum for work ethics seemed to swing in the other direction during the sixties and seventies. Now, work was not something a person did to survive; it was something a person did to acquire more of the "goodies" for themselves and for their children. Parents wanted something more for their children then what they had, so they gave them things that the kids did not have to work for. It was almost as if "work" became a dirty word. There were, however, people who carried on the slogan, "*I can do it*." I was one of these for the most part of my life and raised my children under the same banner. We worked, yes, but we did not know how to have fun. Work was our "*fun time*."

I saw myself developing the opposite slogan where it came to the tech generation. Now I said, "*I can not do this*." I do not understand the instructions and I feel overwhelmed by my being inapt. I was caught in the middle between two generations. The people who said that they could anything they set their mind to, and the older generation who said that they could not understand the computers or even the new type of phones. My mind just could not seem to understand how to operate these new-fangled devices. I was not sure that I wanted to, either. If it were not for the strong passion to write, I would have not tried to learn. I was being pushed forward, even if at a slow pace. Now, the computer was no longer a luxury, it was a necessity.

Out of desperation, I bought a used computer that was one from the beginning age of computers. (This was all that I could afford). The next thing I did was to sign up for computer classes at the college. I can still remember the fear within me each time I was asked to do something, like start the computer. I did not know how to do the simplest things and a failure mind-set blocked my mind from learning. To the degree that "*I can do it*" was the degree that "I can not do it. I struggled on both sides of this mountain. The fear of not being able to do something pushed hard against my pride that I could do all things. I needed help. The Word says, "*I can do all things in Christ, who strengthens me.*" It did not say that I could do all things that I push myself to do.

When I was young, I loved the teeter-totter. One side would go up to the degree the other side would go down. Trying to bring the pride of "*I can do it,*" down and the fear that I could not do it up was such a challenge. I have not completely overcome either of these two, but the old man is crumbling as I type out this page. God has given me several people to help me learn how to use a phone, do facebook, and some more things that "even a child could do."

God released Mary Renteria and Yvonne Edghill to help proof read the books that God had told me to write, and Jacob Biswell volunteered to help publish them. He also did the cover designs for the books and advertised them on facebook. God Bless, Jacob.

This is a little side note that just happened. I have asked my husband to help around the house, but his remark has been, *"I can't do it. I'm not the housewife."* When he was about three years old, his mother became very ill and stopped being the homemaker. The image of his mother not doing what he thought she should do and his father doing what he thought he should not do, (the rolls of men and women's duties) became a mountain of resentment for him. In order to keep his manhood, which he was fighting to maintain, he would refuse to take care of himself if I was not around. In his mind, it was women's work to cook, feed, care for the house, watch the children, etc. Man's work was to earn the money. Being under such a liability in his growing up, George saw helping around the house as detrimental to his health and ego. The mountain we began to face was this. My *"I can do it"* kept receiving more and more jobs laid on me that used to be George's job but after he got sick and could not do the work (in his mind) my pile of do's became a mountain that I could not maintain.

Now, instead of just doing the "womanly" duties, over the years I had to prune the grapes, irrigate, mow the lawn, wash the cars, changing the oil, fix the irrigation system, do the banking and somehow clean house and shop for food, etc. I could not distinguish what was women's work and men's work any longer. I was neither, just a worker.

For several years, I pushed myself to get everything done inside and outside of the house and while becoming a nurse to George because the *"I can do it"* mentality kept me going until I broke. God was probably waiting for me to let go of some things long before I did. Well, I finally met the straw that broke the camel's back. I had just sat down to rest when George demanded that I put mouthwash in the dog's mouth to stop his bad breath. George was sitting next to the dog; and, the mouthwash was next to George. Yes, I could do it, but so could he. Moreover, I told him so, not quite as gentle as I would like to have. George's reaction was to sleep on the couch all night. My reaction was to let him. In the morning, he got up and fixed his own coffee, which for years he would say," (I cannot fix the coffee). The power of his 'can't' have been challenging my "can" for years. That is when I saw the image of Rosie the Riveter on a water jug that I had. This mountain of *"I can do it"* was coming down. I can do only what is God's plan for me to do. *"Rosie, you're crumbling*!

I am sure that you have heard about generation curses. What this means to me is, like mother like daughter. Every time George would say to our daughter *"it's man's work"* she would be determined that *"She could do it."* Traci not only finished college, got her master's degree, worked the night shift at a packing house at fourteen, worked for the post office, worked for the agriculture department, worked at several jobs putting herself through college, learned how to fly an airplane, received her pilots license, took classes to handle guns, and learned to drive the tractor. Now, how do you divide this up into male and female rolls? Traci now holds a master's in business and education.

The spirit of oppression worked hard against us. George believed the lie that if he got up and helped himself; he would be doing the very thing that he hated about his mother and father. Unknown to himself, he was fighting a battle for manhood while despising the roll of the woman. He honestly believed that if women did not bring in money then they had to do all the work around the house as *"their duty."* I resisted this spirit for years, often repenting for taking on jobs that the Lord did not give me, only to boast my thinking, *"I can do it."*

While I am writing this section of the book, I saw a vision of my Aunt Flora. Aunt Flora would get up around four AM, start a pan of bread, haul in the wood for the cooking stove, plant a garden, can the produce of the garden, keep up the house, tend to church and the hundreds of young men and women who got lost in the "Jesus Movement." She worked, worked, and worked. That is, until she fell and ruptured her spleen. She had also been having trouble with her heart that forced her to rest. Rest was not something that she could submit to.

Because of a prolonged rest, Aunt Flora gave up trying to get stronger. She had never been weak in her life. Not knowing how to rest, she went into a desponded condition in which she received the lie, *"I might as well die,"* which she did. She just gave up hope of being able to work again. I write this in hopes of showing that on the one side of the pendulum is a person who does not know how to rest. On the other side of the pendulum is the person who does not know how to work. Both sides become a mountain of self that needs to crumble. Faith without works is dead. Work by itself is dead works. When asked by Jesus' disciples what was the work that they needed to do, Jesus replied, *"To know the Father."* This is truly a work, as it involves learning to listen to the Holy Spirit, reading the Word of God, and obedience to the Word given to them.

God send help! During this last year of dialysis and countless surgeries, the Veterans sent us a "worker" who would help caring for George. At first, I didn't know how to receive the help as the mindset that it was my duty to care for the house and George was so strong. Finally, I realized that I was not strong enough and that I couldn't do everything that needed to be done. My pride of work and strength had to crumble. I had to learn to receive help and be thankful for it.

Chapter 10
Rewards

When I was in the third grade, my parents lived in a small town called Woodacre. My parents bought a small house situated midway up a hill. To me, this hill was a big mountain. It was not until I re-visited my old homestead after I was married that I saw the hill where we once lived only to see that it was a small bump in the road. I was so shocked to see how small this hill was. Anyway, all the kids on the hill had to walk down the hill just like us in order to catch the school bus. That was not too bad. However, the school bus returned to the same location at the bottom of the hill after school ended. Now we had to walk up the hill to return to our home.

I can still remember the game I would play in my mind. I would stand at the bottom of the hill, look up at my parent's house on top of the hill, and visualize my mother having treats for us when we got home. She would make chocolate cookies, cakes, homemade bread, and many goodies. I would visualize myself eating the deserts as my reward for climbing the hill. I would then look at myself at the bottom of the hill. I would say, *"I am at present at the bottom of the hill, but my future is at the top of the hill."* When I get to the top of the hill, I will look at my past at the bottom of the hill. I called the game, past, present, and future. Seeing my future had the power to push me up the hill, day after day, after day.

I did not know that I was opening a door to my soul, called a rewards system. Each time I overcame something, I rewarded myself with a treat. If I worked hard, I got a treat. So, on and so on.

One day, while at a party, someone gave me a prophetic word. *"Because you loved righteousness and hated iniquity, God, your God, will reward you. He is a rewarder of those who diligently seek Him."* Well, the race was on. I had been trained to strive for rewards. Now God promised to reward me if I would diligently seek His face, which I did. Are you beginning to get the picture of the teeter-totter? On one side of the board was my reward in the flesh for accomplishing things. On the other side of the teeter-totter were the rewards for diligently seeking God. One side fed my flesh. The other side fed my spirit. One side had to crumble. I decided to let the gratification to be rewarded with treats fall. I wanted to climb the mountain of faith.

'By faith Abraham, when he was called to go out into a place which he should after receive for an inheritance, obeyed; and he went out, not knowing whether he went." *"But without faith it*

is impossible to please him: for he that cometh to God must believe that he is and that he is a rewarder of them that diligently seek him." (Hebrews 11)

God promised King David that he would bless his generations as a reward for David's love toward God. If I wanted God to bless my family, I had to have something spiritual as my reward. This is where the writings of books came in. I wanted to leave a legacy to my children and my grandchildren with the Word of the Lord. I wanted them to see what God had been doing in my life and hoped that they would be encouraged to seek His face.

Chapter 11
Grumble,

You read it right, the word is grumble, not crumble. Traci and I had been making plans to attend Andrew Womack's 2017 July's conference in Colorado. I arranged with my neighbor to walk the dogs and check on my husband. The route would be through Las Vegas. Just planning the journey stirred up memories of something that had happened twelve years earlier. At that time, Traci had a twelve-year-old Mazda. We planed on visiting Brice Canyon and Zion National Park, and other things of interests. Her car was old, but in good condition, we thought. Knowing the area was extremely hot in July, we packed several gallons of water in the car, just in case. All seemed to be a "go."

Just past Los Vegas, the Mazda started to overheat. We stopped several times to replenish the water in the radiator as the car was over-heating. The car could not take the extreme heat of the desert. As soon as we could, we took the car to a garage only to learn that it appeared that the block was busted. Our vacation came to an abrupt end. After much wrestling with the question, "What should we do?" Traci decided to rent a U Haul truck and return home. Traci loved her car and was not about to abandon it. The drive home, in hundred-degree weather, was extremely nerve-wracking. She had neve driven a U Haul before and the traffic through Las Vega was horrendous. Needless to say, fear and stress became a strong mountain. We never broke into joy, only a feeling of defeat.

Now, thirteen years later, and with another twelve-year old car, an Avalon, we were making plans to visit the Parks that we did not see twelve years earlier. Traci was considering taking her car on the same trip through the desert to Colorado. The old feelings that we thought were dormant arose as a mountain of fear, so much so, that we struggled as to whether to go or not. Traci did all the right things. She took her car into the garage to fix everything possible and service it. Still, there was a spirit of foreboding. We began to consider the wisdom of taking an old car through the desert. We prayed, and prayed, and prayed. The thought came; maybe it would be wisdom to rent a new car. I agreed. I did not want to go through the same experience of having car trouble, again. The temperature was over 100 degrees and being stranded in the desert was not my idea of a vacation.

As I agreed with the idea to rent a car, plans were made. Traci's neighbor would take us to the airport. We arrived t the car rental place before the appointment time and were told that we would just have to wait twenty minutes until our pick-up time unless we signed up to be a preferred customer. We decided to wait. When they released the car, which was to be a non-smoking car, we could not stand the smell of cigarettes. There was no way we could drive this car for four days.

This was our first mountain of grumble that we faced. It was hard to say, *"Praise the Lord,"* but we did. Now, we had to unload this car, pack our suitcases all of the way to the office, in the heat of the day, in order to exchange it for another car. This next car was a mini car and extremely uncomfortable, but we decided to *"Suck it up"* and start our journey. We drove out of the lot determined to have a good time. As we turned the corner, a sprinkler from a near-by business came on and squirted the window. Traci turned on the windshield wipers, only to see that they were broken. We turned around, went back to the rental office, unloaded our luggage, and attempted to get another car, only to be told that they would not give us one. They were not going to take out of commission this car on the busiest weekend of the year, which was the 4h of July. Traci told them that we were going into areas known for thundershowers and it was a necessity to have windshield wipers that worked. "*Too bad.*" If she would not sign up to be a preferred customer, then she could just go home.

The mountain of grumble faced us once again. What this meant was that we could not arrive at the hotel that we had made reservations for, and for which we paid in advance. She had reserved three hotels for the three-day journey giving her credit card as "*good faith.*" If we cancelled all of the hotels, we could be out almost $1,000. Fear was mounting fast. Our insides were like a volcano wanting to erupt in grumble, but we turned to the Lord and praised Him each time.

The only thing that we could do was to call Traci's neighbor to come back and get us. Kristi was such a good sport. She had not been feeling well herself but made the two trips to Fresno for us. It was now late in the day and any thought of arriving at our first destination was gone. Traci notified the motel regarding our dilemma. "*Too bad.*" "*We will not refund your money.*" In the morning, we would have to decide whether to cancel the trip or trust God that the things that had happened in the past would not happen to us now. This was a big deal as the incident stirred up all the memories of the past event in which Traci's car overheated in Las Vegas. What would we do if this car, a car twelve years old, could not make it through he extreme heat of the desert?

After a night of struggling with the memories of the past and the fears of possible car trouble, we decided that we had to face the giant that stood against our trip. We would take Traci's car and praise the Lord for being there with us. What a relief it was when we passed Las Vegas without any trouble.

The first night's rest was at Capitol Reef. What an awesome sight. We could not stop praising God. The next day's stop was in Breckenridge in which we got the best room in the hotel. The suite overlooked the mountains. Everything looked perfect. It was time to eat dinner and settle in for a good night's rest.

At dinner, the waiter came to take our order. Both Traci and I decided on the scallops. Traci asked the waiter if she could get hers without pepper. "No problem." When it was time to be served, the waiter brought out the bread dishes (two of them). Then the waiter brought out one dish of scallops. "Where is the other order? Traci asked. "Oh, you wanted to eat also?" "Maybe I can see if the chef can find something for you." "Never mind," said Traci, "we will share this one order." "What about the bread?" "Did you want bread, said the waiter?" Maybe I can find some in the kitchen."

Traci asked, "Why then did you bring out the bread dishes if bread did not come with the order?" "Oh, that was just to complete the place setting."

It was easy to laugh now. The mountain of "grumble" was coming down. What else could go wrong? We were to find out the next morning. When we left the lodge, we had to drive up to the summit. The car started to over heat and a smell (like paint remover or acetone) became so strong that fear raised his ugly head. The thought of the car breaking down on the summit with no help for miles and the thought of loss to the car came to confront us. That morning we had heard a pastor speak on how fear binds us from taking our authority. We repented for fear, took our authority over it, and continued up and over the mountain, praising God and pushing back the feelings of fear. In the next town, we stopped at several garages for help. They were too busy. One, however, took the time to look at the engine. He did not see any problems, but thought it might be a hole in one of the hoses. We would have to take it to a Toyota dealership in Colorado Springs, which we did. The only thing they found was that the cabin filter was dirty, so they replaced it, (For $250.00). I think they sprayed the car with an air freshener to make us think that the problem was fixed. In order to check out the car, we had to miss a couple of neetings at the conference. We chose not to grumble. That night I awoke at one-thirty in the morning with a word from the Lord. *"Map out a route to return to California."* This meant that we would not return home by way of New Mexico and Arizona. It was not too long afterward that the smell had returned. The original problem was still with us and Las Vegas was before us. If we left right then, we would travel through the desert at night. The temperature was over one hundred degrees. Traci drove straight through from Colorado to home in about eighteen hours. We were so tired but home safe and the car in tact. The next morning Traci called. *"Do you want to know what the smell was?"* She had cleaned the car out completely only to find that the touch-up paint that she had bought and placed inside the glove compartment had exploded! Praise God. He took us to confront Goliath and all the stress, which came with the *"healing"* process. We were able to let fears go and overcome the spirit of grumbling, even temporarily. God was faithful to return us to trusting in Him during high tense moments when everything looked like it could end in disaster.

Chapter 12
Fear of Being Good.

The goodness of God leads to repentance. If a person is afraid of seeing things that he is doing wrong he will be afraid of being good. A good man will lay down his life for his neighbor. A good man will meet the needs of his wife. A good man will seek the Lord for his house. A good man will desire to walk in the presence of God. However, if one is afraid of taking on responsibilities classified as serving others, then fear of being good pushes him over to the other side of the pendulum. This person will be negative in speech and actions. A negative spirit becomes the mountain he will have to overcome and cause to crumble.

I use to pride myself on being a positive person, one who looks to the bright side of life and encourages others that things will get better and say, *"The darkness is just before the dawn."* I had a wrong self-image of my being a positive person. That is until God opened my eyes to see how negative I really was. I will start with a story about our brand-new car.

Several years ago, just after buying a new car, a beautiful maroon car with matching cloth covered seats, George nd I went on vacation to the coast. At that time, George smoked. I could see the ashes on his cigarettes getting longer and longer. I just knew that they would drop on the seat and burn a hole in the fabric. I warned. Yes, I was faithful to warn. *"George, put out the cigarette."* *You're going to drop ashes on the seat."* Of course, George paid no attention and just as I predicted, the ashes dropped right between his legs onto the seat burning a hole in the fabric.

There was another time that I remember so well. We were to attend a wedding in which our daughter was the bride's maid of honor. We had traveled several hours and George wanted a cup of coffee. *"George, be careful, you might spill the coffee on your new shirt."* Guess what. He did. The coffee stains showed up clearly on his beige shirt. I was so angry. I felt that the trip was ruined and I blamed George for all of these things. After all, I warned him of things that could happen. Well, you have the idea. My words were negative! Me, negative? Not me! Yes, me. The only thing that I released was a spirit of shame. None of my warnings changed George to seek God's wisdom. Nothing that I said released God's goodness. What it did do was to build a mountain of fear that George would do something wrong. I never dreamed that what I said would build a mountain of fear in George to do anything good. As I am looking at this mountain, I am repenting for my warnings from fear. A wife is to build up he husband, not tear him down. I did not like someon telling me all of my bad habits, yet I sowed and reape seeds of shame.

When we leave a place of bondage in order to hear from the Holy Spirit, we become a voice to lead others from the law of "*cause and affect.*" We can still see things that can g wrong; however, we are to speak words that protec others from bad things happening to them.
For this mountain to crumble, (a negative spirit), on must repent for seeing everything that can go wrong an speaking it out. We were created to see God's glory, Hi goodness, and the good things that we are entitled t receive. When we do not see that which is in us, we draw the same spirit to us as an attack. Then, while unde attack, we defend our actions by becoming angry with others.

For the next fifteen years I worked hard at changing. ignored the fact that we will all face an opportunity to see if we overcame the very thing that we have been repenting. My opportunity came a couple of days o George's surgery to place a graft in his arm. He wanted coffee, so, like a dutiful wife gave him a cup of hot coffee.

As I pulled out of our driveway some of the coffee spilled on his hand which shocked him so much that he dumped the rest of the coffee on the floorboard of the car. This time my reaction was different. I politely told him that I knew that fear and anger rose up when he got burned but there was a better way of handling the situation. I was so proud of my reaction as I remembered my first reactions years earlier. Eureka, I made it.

Chapter 13
It's Only Paint

The phrase, *"its only paint"* refers to a slogan I learned from my mother. It means, *"Don't get upset or worry about mistakes,"* We can re-do the situation and turn things around. My mother's favorite statement was, *"All things work together for good to those who love God."* She had faith that God could turn that which looked like a disaster into praise.

One of the things I remember regarding this phrase is this. Mom bought a goose from a neighbor and planned to cook it for the family. She had already killed the goose plucked out the feathers, gutted the innards, and was ready to fry the goose when something came up to divert her attention. I remember my mother telling me that she fed the guts to the cats and placed the goose in the icebox until she had time to fry it. When she was about ready to cook the bird, she noticed that the cats that ate the guts had died. Mom threw the goose away and praised God for saving the family. Instead of looking at being distracted from cooking, Mom said, *"All things work together for those who love God."* The loss of money was then *"It's only paint."* Mom put more value in trusting God then allowing herself to become angry or fearful for he things that did not turn out as she planned.

his phrase became a lifesaver to me and to my daughter who picked up the saying. Whenever a mountain of fear f making a mistake that would cost us money arose, we vould say, *"It's only paint."* Then, we would see this fear f loss of finances crumble.

Chapter 14
Alters

The definition of the word "alter" means to change. The "alters" that I am speaking about is in regards to a change in one's personality due to a trauma that changes a person's personality into that of another personality.

The first recorded alter is in the story of Adam and Eve. God created Adam and Eve in His image and in His likeness. The moment Eve gave herself to disobey God, her personality changed. Both Adam and Eve became fearful, ashamed, and conscious of the separation between them and God. In this "new" state or personality (being carnal) they began to control the situation by sewing fig leaves together to deal with shame. Because of the trauma, they were separated from the Garden of Eden, the place God had prepared for them.

God does not leave us in a separated condition. He offers a way back to Him, which is through the blood covenant. Today, we have the same offer of restoration, the Blood of Jesus, which is the only way back to the Father's presence.

For years, I have been aware of different personalities rise in my life. I was not sure how to handle these personalities. I had attended a class that dealt with the four types of personalities, the sanguine, the phlegmatic, the melancholic, and the choleric. The sanguine is a person who is very optimistic, hopeful, buoyant, confident, and cheerful. The phlegmatic person is unemotional and serene, tranquil, calm, and composed. The melancholic personality has feelings of sadness and depressions while the choleric person is bad-tempered, angry, cranky, crabby, touchy, and short temper with extreme irritable.

At one of the seminars, I took a test to see into what category I would find myself. Under certain conditions, I responded in all four groups almost equally while my husband was a dominant phlegmatic. When I would respond to any of the three groups that differed from him, his strength of being a phlegmatic would pull me into that personality. When I was around a person who was a sanguine, either I became happy and joyful or I went to the extreme of being jealous of the person and responded as a choleric. Noticing these personality changes, I began to call upon the blood of Jesus to help me become the person whom He created me to be.

It was not until I was in mid-life that I began to sense a complete "other" person emerge. This "other" personality acted like that of a child. I attended another conference, this time by "French" who spoke on dealing with the demonic spirits and the alter spirits. When I first introduced myself to him, his first response was, "*You have a child alter.*" Okay, now what was I to do? After the meeting, I asked God for a Scripture. John 17 came to my thoughts. Jesus was praying that we become one with the Father, as we are one with Him. I began to speak to this alter to come to Jesus and receive His blood. I was challenged as to how to bring this alter to a place of maturity.

Now, here I am in my "golden years." I became concerned by the "personality" changes in my husband. He no longer presents himself as the phlegmatic person. On the contrary. Now is responds to almost everything in a fearful negative manner. His responses became that of anger, hate, jealous, resentment, etc. These responses were met by corresponding responses from me, most unlike the response of Jesus to love the unlovely. After about seventeen years of hand-to-hand combat, I began to see a pattern. These were alters speaking because of traumatic events that occurred while he was dealing with cancer in his body and chemical changes due to kidney failure. Personalities and alters were expressing themselves multiple times in a day and I wondered where "George" was hiding. Someone else was in control.

At another seminar by George Freeman, the Spirit told me that I was dealing with three separate alters, none of which knew the Lord. My first encounter was with the "child" alter while at the Veterans Hospital during the time in which his kidneys began to hemorrhage. The family, being concerned and supportive of us, came to visit George. All was great for a few minutes, George was back (not the child alters). Then, when the doctor asked the family to wait in the hall while they examined the patient in the adjoining bed, the child-alter emerged transforming George's appearance. The family had never seen this before and they became concerned. I asked them to join me in introducing this alter to Jesus. George began to cry like a child and did not want to ask Jesus into his heart. He wanted me to do it for him. I encouraged him that he was the one who had to do the asking. After a few minutes, he spoke to Jesus and the child alter disappeared.

A few hours later, George was dismissed from the hospital and another alter appeared but I did not know how to handle this one. This one was a strong and domineering personality who took control of the situation. It was as if no one could touch him. Two months later, I attended another conference by George Freeman. That night I was shown that I had three alters that matched George's three alters. They are, the child, the one who controls, and the sexual alter. When the alter personality of control was in charge, George would rule the situations he faced by fear, jealousy, and hatred. All of these responses stirred the same spirits in me. Of course nothing good came of our conflict. However, God gave me as scripture in Psalm 136, "*Give thanks, His love endures forever.*" God so loved George and I that He gave His Son to die for us. I needed this love to respond in the situations that arose. I had to change in order for these alters to crumble.

That weekend God showed me in a vision His hand reaching through my side and bringing out a "blob" of something. I asked the Lord what this was and was taken back in time to when I was about three years old. I was taking a bath in the washtub when I felt a blob come toward me and enter me. I felt the weight of this blob but did not know what it was or how it affected me. I sought God for answers over the years but to no avail. This last year I learned that it was a sexual spirit. To counter the sexual spirit, a timid alter that was afraid of sex emerged.

George encountered this same alter when as a teen, he asked a girl out on a date, but was refused. A lie entered that he would never get married because no one wanted him. During one of his surgeries, the doctors had to remove his prostate. Now, the fear of losing his power to keep me rose to control by hate, jealousy, and bitterness. God had reminded me of a children's book, "*Peter Piper Pumpkin Eater, had a wife but couldn't keep her, so he put her in a pumpkin shell, and there he kept her very well.*" George did not turn to God for help. Instead, he blamed God for the lack of sex and turned to these other spirits in order to keep under control the things he feared that he would lose.

A short time after this last conference, the Lord showed me in a vision a picture of the "Incredible Hulk." He said that trauma often causes the cells in the brain to split allowing alters to be formed. If you remember the movie about the "Hulk" whenever pain or anger was in control, David, the scientist, was transformed into the Hulk. I asked God what I was to do. I heard, Psalm 42. In this Psalm, King David asks his soul, "*Soul, why are you discomforted, praise God.*"

It was this same weekend of the seminar that I saw the mountain of alters begin to crumble. They have not all come down, but they will. I remembered the word at Bethel, Redding years ago, "*you will climb a stock like Jack in the Bean Stock, but you will not kill "Jack." He will crumble a the feet of Jesus.*" During this weekend, I saw a "Cousin Jack" hat on top of a tall fig tree. I knew that the fig tree represented my body, soul, and spirit. I believed that the interpretation was a fulfillment of the word given to me at Bethel. "Jack" (the alters that were in control) were coming down! They would submit to Jesus and become one with Him, healed, whole, and set free.

Late Monday afternoon after a day of much prayer and praise, I received two scriptures. Isaiah 6:1 "*In the year Uzziah died I saw the Lord sitting upon a throne, high and lifted up, and his train filled the temple*" and Isaiah 35, which is a promise of restoration and joy. Then, in an open vision, I saw myself being clothed in a green dress. looked up the biblical meaning and learned that it mean resurrection power. Therefore, here I am, the new resurrected, Birdie. I do not know how this will look in the years to come, but I have begun to rest in "My New Creation."

Chapter 15
Unforgiveness

My Dad would tell us kids of an incident on Pango Pango in which a Japanese torpedo hit the island. Dad would recall that at about 2 A.M. the family was awakened by the noise of being bombed. My oldest brother, Ken, remembered running out of the house toward a building barefoot. He said that he still remembers the rocks cutting his feet. Dad remembers grabbing his pants as his wallet was in the back pocket, and then taking another one of my brothers, Jack, in his arms as they ran for this same building. My Mom carried my brother, Byron, who was about six months old.

I paid little attention to the stories as they seemed to be embellished as the years went by. For some reason, (I am going to say that it was God) I felt led to Google Pango Pango. To my surprise, Dad was pretty accurate in what had happened. The report was the following:

'On January 11, 1942, at 2:26 a.m., a Japanese submarine surfaced off Tutuila between Southworth Point and Fagasa Bay and fired about 15 shells from its 5.5-inch deck gun at the U.S. Naval Station Tutuila over the next 10 minutes. The first shell struck the rear of Frank Shimasaki's store, ironically owned by

one of Tutuila's few Japanese residents. The store was
closed, as Mr. Shimasaki had been interned as an enemy alien.
The next shell caused slight damage to the naval dispensary, th
third landed on the lawn behind the naval quarters known a.
"Centipede Row," and the fourth struck the stone seawal
outside the customs house. The other rounds fell harmlessl
into the harbor. As one writer described it, "The fire was no
returned, notwithstanding the eagerness of the Samoar
Marines to test their skill against the enemy... No American o.
Samoan Marines were wounded."

As I continued my search for information, I learned tha
God had spared my family from almost certain deatl
twice. Once was from the bombing and the other wa:
from being executed by the Japanese on Wake.

My Dad, while employed as a construction worker by
Morris-Knudson Construction out of Boise, Idaho, wa:
sent to Wake Island then transferred to American Samoar
Islands just months before the island was captured. It wa:
while stationed on Pango Pango (building housing for the
military) that my family, consisting of my mother and
father and three brothers were almost killed by the above-
mentioned bomb.

The night after reading the above article I dreamed that I
was missing something. When I awoke, I asked God what

was. I was told to pray for the families of all the construction workers who were killed on Wake. They were still grieving and it was time for closure. My family was one of the lucky ones who left Wake before the Japanese took the island. The news article mentioned that for each year after the war survivors from Wake and their families would meet for a reunion in Boise. This was the last year. I began to pray for closure for all of these victims. It was time for the mountain of sorrow that they were feeling to crumble. I was so honored to be a part of God's plan to speak healing to those still hurting. To do this, I had to address an inward hatred for my father as well. I had made judgments against him for putting my family in harms way and justifying his actions by saying, "I had to make money." In God's grace, the Holy Spirit brought forth the rejoicing that God spared our family and forgave me for my attitude.

Seth Randall, the reporter for M-K, went the second mile in his efforts to find out things about my dad during that time. He sent me a newspaper clipping stating that my dad had taken out a license to promote a boxer. I never knew that. I copied the article and sent it to my children as a "keepsake" for their children. I was then able to make a time-line of my life that I had placed out of my mind. The Lord showed me so many times in which I held judgment against my dad and was finally able to confront these and ask God to forgive me. After reading John 16 and Psalm 122, stating that it was time to go to the house o the Lord with a glad heart, I finally received my dad with a glad heart. It only took me seventy years.

I looked up the word glad, and it meant to rejoice for and over another so that God's presence could bless "them (me and my father). In John 16 Jesus sends the Holy Spiri to convict of sin (my lack of gladness over others), o Righteousness, (Jesus made us righteous through Hi Blood), so that we could enter the Father's presence with a glad heart. Now, in His presence, we had the right to ask the Father, and keep asking the Father, to bless other so that they could be set free in their heart. That is what did, I asked God to bless all the families from Wake to be free in their heart and to be able to forgive.

Chapter 16
The Bicycle

I received my first bicycle at seven years if age, (with the following instructions). *"If a car comes toward you, you are to get off the bicycle until it passes."* Well, I started out obeying the rule for at least the first few minutes, and then I realized that there were so many cars coming toward me that I would never ride the bike at all. I determined right then that this rule was unfounded and that I could not carry it out and ride my bike.

Today, if a person rides a bicycle on the rode, the law says that he is to ride with traffic. This was not the case when I was seven. The law said those who rode a bike or who were a pedestrian were to walk against traffic. I like this law better as I could see the traffic coming toward me and not be surprised from behind.

After all these years, I can still hear the threats from my father that if I did not obey, He would take my bicycle away from me. Fear entered which caused great trouble in the years to come. Fear of losing my bike became a mountain that I would have to face years later.

I spoke earlier about my living in Tamales when I first told God that I loved Him. I looked up a report on the town only to learn that there were approximately 200 residence in the 2010 censes, so you can image how small this town was when I was there in 1952. As the traffic was limited, I felt free to stay on my bike for long periods without dismounting even though I was in total disobedience to my dad.

On one particular day, I confronted a trauma that almost cost me my life. I was returning home from town when I came to a "Y" section in the road. Now, because of the split in the road, I found myself on the wrong side of the road as I was taking the turn to the left. I still remember the instructions given to me by my father, *"Ride on the left side of the road."* To do this, I would have to cross the road at the point of intersection. The road was on a downhill curve, so I was unable to see any cars coming up from the other side. The moment I made the decision to cross over to the other side I saw the oncoming car coming toward me. I applied my brakes in time only to skid under the front of the car. I do not know who was more afraid, the woman driving the car, my self, or the fear that my dad would take my bike from me if he learned of the accident. (I decided not to tell him).

It seems that only a few months passed when my folks decided to move from Tamales to Rincon Valley, a small own outside of Santa Rosa. My folks rented several acres of land, stocked it with milking cows, and went into the dairy business. I was too young to do much help so I entertained myself riding carefree around the loop in the valley floor. I felt so free, my face to the wind, my mind in the clouds, and my feet on the pedals. What Dad did not know, did not hurt him. He was too busy trying to survive to check on me as to whether I dismounted my bike every time a car came toward me.

My freedom was short lived. The dairy business failed, my bike was sold for food, and Dad was out of work again. Just before we left the place in Rincon Valley, my Dad made a small "shack" from left over wood from his contracting business. My parents found a lot for rent across from Santa Rosa High School in which to place the shack. The shack became "*Leola's Hamburger Stand.*" Next-door was a small house that we rented. Dad had promised me that he would buy me another bike (he sold my bike to buy food) ... someday. Well, he did keep his word. My next bike was one that was used, so I did not have the passion for it as I did for the one, he sold, as it was brand new. Well, I did have a bike, for a few days. Within the first few weeks of school, someone slashed the tires on my bike and there was not any money to buy another tube. I cried for days. I was given the bike so that I could leave school on an early lunch break, ride to the hamburger shake to work, then ride back to school. That was the plan. But now, without a bike, things would have to change. Now, Byron and I had to run to get to the hamburger stand in time to work.

Everyone was expected to help with this new venture. Mom would get up around two in the morning to start a batch of donuts that she sold for five cents. After the donuts were ready, she made the pies while dad made the hamburgers and hot dogs having them ready for the noon rush. Jack was in charge of the cokes, ice cream, etc. Byron and I would take the money.

I cannot remember having a bike again until I was married. Then, as "luck" would have it, while riding by the Reedley High School, a car passed another car and not seeing me, we collided. My bike hit the front left tire of his car damaging my new bike. Fortunately, the insurance company replaced my bike with another "brand new" one, which I have to this date.

Here I am, August 9, 2017, when I received a word from the Lord. I was to go back to the time when I was seven years old and repent for disobedience, for making a false judgment against the instructions I was given, and for an attitude of rebellion that I had against my father, and enounce the fear of losing my bicycle. As I did these, he Lord brought my attention to a book written by Stacy). Hillard called "*A Return to Sonship*" published by True 'otential. On page 96 it says,

Jesus is not God's adopted Son, but rather His only begotten on, God's eternal plan for mankind. While the Bible clearly tates that Jesus is God's "only" begotton Son, it also refers to esus as the "Firstbegotton." "The Bible links this status of first egotton to Jesus' return into the world as indicative of the fact hat they occur simultaneously. At Jesus' return, we will be hanged from our present state into His glorious state by the edemption of our bodies.

Vhat this means to me is that once I repent for the fears hat entered me regarding my bicycle, and return to my 'ather as did the prodigal son in Luke 15, then my status s changed to being one with the firstbegotton Son, which s the glorification of resurrected life.

Vhile estranged from God in any area, that area does not ;lorify God and has no power to reclaim health, healing, tc. for flesh and blood cannot inherit the kingdom of 3od (I Corinthians 15:50). My inheritance depends on my 'elationship to the Father through being One with Jesus n each area that I was estranged from Him. Therefore, 1ow that I addressed the mountain of "bicycle" I have legal rights to reclaim all that was lost.

Chapter 17
Unrequited Love.

The definition for unrequited love is either love that is not received or not reciprocated by the person you love or a love that is not known by a secret admirer.

One of Jacob Biswell's prophetic words to me was, *"God is going to tie up some loose ends to set you free in your ministry."* Do you not just love a word that is given to you in which you do not have the least understanding? Well, I didn't know what God was going to do in order to tie up those ends, and my mind decided to take off on a whirlwind trying to figure it out ... to no avail, of course. Then, as I was listening to Jonathan Cahn's teaching on the crucifixion of Jesus, he spoke on the meaning of Jesus saying, *"I thirst."*

He said that there comes a time in which we are to bring something to Jesus (that is as bitterness in our soul) so that we can be healed in that area. This act was *"tying up loose ends."* Immediately I stopped and asked the Holy Spirit just what lose end did I need to bring to Jesus. I heard, Acts 4. Peter and John were teaching in the Temple and telling about the resurrection of Jesus to the Sadducees, the priests, and the people just how much

Jesus loved them. He loved them enough to die for them. The message was not received. In fact, they pu Peter and John into prison and forbade them to speak ir the name of Jesus ever again. After I read Acts 4, I hearc the word, "*Unrequited love*." Immediately I asked the Holy Spirit just what this meant.

The Lord began to video something in my mind that had said when I was about seven. I said, "*I do not think my Dad loves me.*" He was so negative. He never did what want to do; only what he wanted to do. I then concluded "*If dad did not love me, then why should I love him.*" This is a perfect example of unrequited love and the solutions we come up with in order to handle rejection. We reject the person and place them in a prison of our own making For me, I became estranged, cut off from ever wanting tc feel love toward my father. We might live in the same house, and I would obey his rules, but that was all. I consoled myself with the fact that my mother loved me and my brother loved me. That would have to be enough.

It is funny how we desire to imprison those whom we feel do not love us. This desire only brings us into the bondage of loneliness. God has to come to us in that area in His Righteousness and Love until we cry out to Him, "*I'm thirsty to drink from the well of Living Water.*" "*Come,*

ord Jesus. *Restore life and love to me once again.*" By faith,
saw myself released from the prison of being confined in
ny emotions and mind. I opened my heart to receive the
esurrected Jesus to give me a new heart.

Chapter 18
Tuft

If anyone has ever had a "most favorite" pet and had tha
pet die, then you will know soul's emotional trauma.
had such a dog. My daughter found Tuft and his siste
(Shelby) fourteen years ago in a plum orchard. They wer
only a few days old, sick, abandoned, and all alone. Tuf
had mange all over his body with just a "tuft" of hair or
his ears. I was repulsed to look at him in that condition
There was no way that I wanted him. Had not Traci beer
so protective and compassionate over animals, I woulc
not have had anything to do with him, except that we
could see something inside of Tuft that was so special.

Traci took Tuft to the Veterinary, and he too, saw
something special. Tuft was worth the cost to save. O:
course, he wasn't going to give his services free, bu
encouraged Traci to have him treated. Traci couldn't keep
both puppies', she already had a large dog. We, too, had a
larger dog, Chester, whom we already loved
Nevertheless, there was always room for one more. It was
decided, each of us would take a puppy.

I was surprised when my husband said that he would
take the "male." Tuft was so needy that a lot of attention

nd love would have to be poured into him. That was o be my job. Traci paid the financial end while we to the esponsibility of caring. Once his hair started to grow, so lid my love for him. Before the hair grew, however, he ooked like a rat and I was so against rats.

As soon as Tuft and Shelby were able to walk, we began aking them with us as we would walk almost every day. t wasn't long before I knew that there was something so pecial about Tuft. He had an anointing of love that just aptured your heart, and the heart of our neighbors.

would love to say that Tuft was so obedient that that vas why we loved him. That was not the case. Tuft was ust Tuft. He would do his own thing marching to the peat of his own little drum. He walked around like he vas so happy and in love with the world. You could liscipline him for wetting on the carpet, but he refused to :hange. Nevertheless, you put up with him. He was love ind he stole our heart.

During the fourteen years of our relationship, Tuft struggled with rotten teeth, a heart murmur, and kidney problems. Through it all, he was a trooper. I would hold nim close to my chest just as I would my own baby. Each ime that he would get sick, we would pray over him. I would have visions that he would die and immediately take him before the Lord for life. On one occasion, when his body was swollen, I took him to our prayer group to have other lay hands on him, which they did. Trying to keep Tuft alive as a long process. On one occasion, I felt the life of Tuft flow out of him. I held him tightly to my heart and prayed. In the middle of the night George woke me, telling me that he, too, was praying that God would spare him. In the morning, Tuft was his happy self. We did have to have water removed from his lungs and give him heart pills and water pills. All of which we were willing to do, pay the cost, to keep him alive. He was that precious to us.

Well, this last episode in which Tuft received medicine for his heart,went on for about six months when his heart began to fail again. I took him back to the Veterinary only to be told that he was in hospice. The Vet offered to put Tuft asleep, but knew that I was not ready for that, my soul was still hanging on to life.

I was told to feed Tuft drops of fluid every hour as he was in dehydration, which I did for about six hours. At ten o'clock that night I went to bed. I was awakened by a faint cry coming from the kitchen. The T.V. was on, yet the mother instinct in me could hear the cry of her child. Tuft vas that, my child. I picked him up, held him to my hest once again, and would rock him in the rocker. He vould gasp for breath. I knew that he was in pain. I egan praying for Tuft in tongues and praising God. Each ime that I laid hands on his back and prayed, the cry vould subside. When I moved my hand, the cries began. My soul was crumbling between not wanting him to uffer, (I thought of putting him to sleep to spare him) nd the thought that Jesus was on the cross struggling for reath. In the Scripture, John 12:27, Jesus said that He lidn't want to go through this suffering, but that He vould to please the Father and to save all who would call pon Him for salvation. Jesus paid the supreme price.

During those six hours my soul's travail, I asked the Holy Spirit to show me what I needed to see. I was shown in a vision George's mother holding on to her daughter, who t about two years old, was dying. She had been playing vith a stick in her mouth and fell. The stick infected her mouth and the infection began to spread throughout her vhole body. Penicillin had not yet been invented. For hours she would watch the life of her child leave her body. I don't know how much she had trusted God during this time, as she manifested a mental breakdown hat affected the whole family. I was then taken in the Spirit back in time to release God's Word over her and declare healing, even those she has been physically dead for years. God's Word does not return to Him void He sends out His Word for someone to claim. If one generation doesn't, then another can become the "near kinsman" redeemer for them. This was then, my job, o honor.

After this was accomplished, I released Tuft into the Lord's hand, telling Him that I trusted in Him. My desires for tuft to stay with us would have to crumble Surrendering to God had to be the ultimate of my love and appreciation for what Jesus went through for us. A four AM I saw in a fraction of time two images. One was of Tuft dying in front of me, the other of Tuft raised up and happy. I knew that the end of natural life was here but that he entered another life ... an eternal life. believed that God took Tuft to heaven, which was so comforting.

I was prepared to bury Tuft myself. It would be hard, but I had to rise up and take responsibility. I called my daughter-in-law if I could bury him on their ranch. She graciously said that Tom our sin, would come and do this for me.

After about a week of mourning, I had a visitation from

Tuft." He was happy, playing with a big dog and a small dog in the yard of my Aunt Mida's, who had been dead for years. He didn't want to come back to earth. He had a better place in which to live. What a comfort for my boss. People often ask if their animals would be in heaven waiting for them. I remember when Roy Roger's horse, Trigger, died. Someone asked him this same question. His answer, "If there are animals in heaven, and there is, then Trigger is there with Him."

There is a chorus that goes something like this, "His love never fails, gives out, never runs out on me." It was so important for me to know that Tuft was in heaven, that God's love for me never runs out. There are times that the things that we hold most dear will have to crumble before a Might God, who has a better plan. In 2 Chronicles 20:6 it says, "O Lord God of our fathers, are You not God in heaven, and do You not rule over all the kingdoms of the nations, and in Your hand is there not power and might, so that no one is able to withstand You?"

There comes a time in everyone's life in which they have to place the things that they love into God's hands, trusting in His power to keep that which is entrusted to Him. Some may have their loved ones returned to them as was in the case of Abraham when he was asked to surrender his only son to God. Then, there are times tha our loved ones are taken home to live with God fo eternity. To be able to completely trust in God, we have t allow our ways to crumble before Him.

Chapter 19
Critical Spirit

One night, in a dream, I was shown two people. I then heard the words, "are you ready to see something that you have held in darkness?" If course, I said, "Yes." A couple of days later, I was directed to a book that said, "Judgment against our thoughts." There comes a time in which God judges the thoughts of man. If we go back in our mind to dote on past loves, then God says that we have committed double whoredoms. The mind is one of the gifts that need to be brought out of the shadow of darkness into the light. If in our thought life we have sinned against another, we are held in darkness until the light comes to set us free. I had been praying for truth, so was willing to see anything that I held in darkness. I was then shown an episode of a conversation between myself and another person fifty years ago. This person was telling me that her husband had committed adultery and that she was unable to forgive him. She asked my thoughts.

Fifty years ago, I did not know anything about redemption, only the law for sinning. On this subject, adultery, I was vehement. There were no excuses. In my mind and heart, I judged the man for adultery but excused the wife when she married another man. I didn't know that this was a critical spirit.

One night, as I was listening to Bill Johnson of Bethel Redding, he said that when we see someone doing something wrong, it is our job to pray for their restoration, not for telling others their sin. My sin of being critical was just as bad as committing adultery as it fed upon the lives of another. I was then impressed to read the story of "The Gingerbread Man."

If you would ask most people if they knew the story of the Gingerbread man, they would say, "Yes." God wanted to use this story as a parable for me to learn something. In Song of Songs, God identifies the foxes as a thief that comes to steal something from us. In my case, it was relationships. How can you have a relationship with someone of whom you are critical? For those who do not know the story of the Gingerbread man, I'll write it out for you.

Once upon a time there was an old man, an old woman, and a little boy. One morning the old woman made some gingerbread in the shape of a man. She added icing for his hair and clothes, and little blobs of dough for his nose and eyes. When she put him in the oven to bake, she said o the little boy, "You watch the gingerbread man while your grandfather and I go out to work in the garden."

So, the old man and the old woman went out and began to dig potatoes, and left the little boy to tend the oven. But he started to day dream, and didn't watch it all of the time. All of a sudden, he heard a noise, and he looked up and the oven door popped open, and out of the oven jumped a gingerbread man, and went rolling along end over end towards the open door of the house. The little boy ran to shut the door, but the gingerbread man was too quick for him and rolled through the door, down the steps, and out into the road long before the little boy could catch him.

The little boy ran after him as fast as he could manage, crying out to his grandfather and grandmother, who heard the noise, and threw down their spades in the garden to give chase too. The gingerbread man outran all three a long way, and was soon out of sight, while they had to sit down, all out of breath, on a bank to rest.

On went the gingerbread man, and by-and-by he came to two men digging a well who looked up from their work and called out, "Where ye going, gingerbread man?" He said, "I've outrun an old man, an old woman, and a little boy - and I can outrun you too-o-o!"

"You can, can you? We'll see about that?" Said they, and so they threw down their picks and ran after him, bu couldn't catch up with him, and soon they had to si down by the roadside to rest.

On ran the gingerbread man, and by-and-by he came to two men digging a ditch. "Where ye going, gingerbread man?" said they.

He said, "I've outrun an old man, an old woman, a little boy, and two well diggers, and I can outrun you too-o-o!" "You can, can you? We'll see about that!" said they, and they too threw down their spades, and ran after him. The gingerbread man soon outstripped them also, and seeing they could never catch him, gave up the chase and sa down to rest.

On went the gingerbread man, and by-and-by he came to a bear. The bear said, "Where are ye going, gingerbread man?"

He said, "I've outrun an old man, an old woman, a little boy, two well diggers, and two ditch diggers, and I can outrun you too-o-o!"

You can, can you?" Growled the bear. "We'll see about that!" He trotted as fast as his legs could carry him after the gingerbread man, who never stopped to look behind him. Before long the bear was left so far behind that he saw he might as well give up the hunt at the start, so he stretched himself out by the roadside to rest.

On went the gingerbread man and by-and-by he came to a wolf. The wolf said, "Where ye going, gingerbread man?"

He said, "I've outrun an old man, an old woman, a little boy, two well diggers, two ditch diggers, and a bear, and I can outrun you too-o-o!"

You can, can you?" Snarled the wolf. "We'll see about that!" So he set into a gallop after the gingerbread man, who went on and on so fast, that the wolf too saw there was no hope of overtaking him, and he too lay down to rest.

On went the gingerbread man, and by-and-by he came to a fox that lay quietly in a corner of the fence. The fox called out in a sharp voice, but without getting up, "Where ye going, gingerbread man?"

He said: "I've outrun an old man, an old woman, a little boy, two well diggers, two ditch diggers, a bear, and a wolf, and I can outrun you too-o-o!"

The fox said, "I can't quite hear you, gingerbread man. Won't you come a little closer?" Turning his head, a little to one side.

The gingerbread man stopped his race for the first time, and went a little closer, and called out in a very loud voice, "I've outrun an old man, an old woman, a little boy, two well diggers, two ditch diggers, a bear and a wolf, and I can outrun you too-o-o."

"I still can't quite hear you. Won't you come a little closer?" Said the fox in a feeble voice, as he stretched out his neck towards the gingerbread man, and put one paw behind his ear.

The gingerbread man came up close, and leaning towards the fox, screamed out "I'VE OUTRUN AN OLD MAN, AN OLD WOMAN, A LITTLE BOY, TWO WELL DIGGERS, TWO DITCH DIGGERS, A BEAR AND A WOLF, AND I CAN OUTRUN YOU TOO-O-O!"

"You can, can you?" Yelped the fox, and he snapped up the gingerbread man in his sharp teeth in the twinkling of an eye. (Story from internet).

his is how the Spirit interpreted this story to me. God ? trying to get out attention but we keep running away rom Him. Time after time He sends someone to correct ιs, but we are too busy doing the things that we want to lo in order to satisfy our flesh. Then, because we haven't ›een listening to God, the devil sends a thief to catch us in . deception. He lets us think that we are so smart, so ;ood, and so indestructible. At first the fox (evil spirit) leceives us into thinking that he really wants to help us .ccomplish something. It's a lie. He then comes a second ime to seduce us again. Finally, when we think that we ιre about to get to where we want to be, we are caught in 1is trap.

As I began to worship God, asking Him for more nstructions, I heard a scripture, Psalm 64. I was not going o miss an experience with the Holy Spirit and neglect His varnings. The concept of this passage says:

'Preserve my life from fear of the enemy. Hide me from he secret plots of the wicked" (Psalm 64:1-2). God was varning me that there was a fox just waiting to open up 1is mouth and swallow me whole. Unless I separated nyself from a past stronghold in my flesh, I would be :aught in a trap that was set for me. That Sunday I shared vith the church and we all repented for a critical spirit and took communion. This critical spirit had to crumble!

Chapter 20 Fear of Punishment

During "Pro-Life's" 40 days of prayer, the organization asked for help in praying for those who would be going to the abortion clinic in Fresno. If they volunteered, there would be certain requirements that need to be met. One was, to be full of love and never have any critical or judgmental spirit. Well, I had just dealt with a critical spirit, so I felt that I was ready to serve God in love for others. I was paired with my pastor, Ataloa, and we walked up and down the sidewalk asking if we could pray for those we met. As it turned out, we had the privilege of speaking into the lives of at least four women who needed help. They were not pregnant, but needed assistance.

One of the ladies was new to the area and wanted to be connected to a local agency that could advise them in different matters. She was a believer and received prayer quite easily. The next person thought that she had a cyst someplace inside and needed to be tested. The third person was looking for a place to stay in order to get her children back. She had found a job but needed a residence. As the pastor prayed for her, she saw in a vision, sunflowers. She didn't know what this meant, only that it was a sign to be considered. This person went on their way north while we continued our walk south. We came to a young student who just spoke up t(pastor, saying, "I plant sunflowers." "See!" She pulled ou her telephone in which she had taken pictures of her priz(possessions. Coincidental? I don't think so. Soo afterward, as we continued our walk, we met the firs land in whom the prophecy was given and introduce(her to the student who was raising sunflower seeds. W(don't know what would transpire, only that God was a work. On the way home I mentioned that I knew that needed to learn something more from God. I needed word that would crumble a false image in my soul.

The Belt Strap

I received a word from the Lord, fear of punishment. was then impressed to read from Hebrews 6. Paul wa: instructing us to do the things that accomplish salvatior and bear fruit for His glory. One of these changes was t(see our self, seated at the Father's right hand, enjoying al of our inheritance given to us by Jesus. I was then told t(read Acts 7 which was a history lesson for the Jews. I wil paraphrase this chapter the way the Holy Spirit impressed me.

Like Abraham, God was calling me out of a darkness in which I served in a bondage. Moses, God's deliver, was

alled to defend and lead God's people, but when he
aw an Egyptian fighting with an Israelite, he killed the
Egyptian. It never occurred to him that the Israelite
would not trust Moses when he saw Moses become so
ngry and want to punish the Egyptian for fighting.
Another story was about Stephen, who, while being
toned for speaking of God's love, said, "Father, forgive
hem."

Moses wanted to punish someone for a wrong. Stephen
wanted God to forgive the persons doing a wrong so that
hey would be reconciled to Him. God reminded me that
 had a bad spirit with my soul that needed to crumble. I
hought people had to be punished when they did
horrible things to others. The lie entered when I was
really young. Whenever I did something my father didn't
ike, He would take his razor strap and snap it as a
warning that I was about to be punished. He would also
raise his arm as if to slap me when I would "horse
around" in the car. Of course, I never got hit or slapped,
ust threatened, that opened a door to believing that
people needed to be punished if they did something
wrong. I was to be like Stephen, pray for others to know
God's love as Jesus took our punishment at the Cross.

Because of what Jesus did, our inheritance is to have the power to liberate those bound, to embrace those who feel estranged from God, and to allow His mercy and grace flow from us to others as living water. We cannot walk in our inheritance as the "New Man" as long as the old man is alive. I did not know that the desire to punish others was a form of abuse. We are called to help correct others where lies prevail. We are called to love where there is hate. Foremost, we are to pray for others that God will forgive them and restore them to fellowship with Him.

Conclusion

Every thought that exalts itself is an idol or a mountain that has to crumble. God will not have another above Him. He alone is the High, Exalted One, and worthy of all praise and glory. Jesus came down to touch our lives so that we could be transformed into His image and bare His likeness and His name. This is the great mystery, Jesus lives in man. It is our job to ask the Holy Spirit to reveal God's plans for our lives so that we can walk on this earth as kings and priests unto Him.

Made in the USA
Columbia, SC
31 March 2019